Celebrating Mothers

Celebrating Mothers

by
Teri Wilhelms
and
Debbie Denton

Rutledge Hill Press®
Nashville, Tennessee
A Thomas Nelson Company

Mothers: A Celebration by Alexandra Stoddard on page 11 copyright © 1996 by Alexandra Stoddard. Used by permission from William Morrow and Company, Inc. Story on pages 39–41 first published in *Good Housekeeping* August 1974. Story on pages 58–61 by Nancy Hall—a freelance writer living in Madison, Conn.—copyright © 2000 by National Public Radio®. Used by permission. Stories on pages 30, 78–81, and 126 from *Nelson's Complete Book of Stories, Illustrations, and Quotes* copyright © 2000 by Robert J. Morgan. Used by permission from Thomas Nelson Publishers, Inc.

Published in Nashville, Tennessee, by Rutledge Hill Press, a Thomas Nelson company, P.O. Box 141000, Nashville, Tennessee, 37214.

ISBN: 1-55853-885-2

Printed in Colombia
1 2 3 4 5 6 7 8 9 — 05 04 03 02 01

Motherlove

Its power is often supernatural. So strong is its magic, in fact, it can make you feel safe in an unsafe world, hopeful in a hopeless situation, inspired in a time in which inspiration is the rarest of all commodities.

—Laura B. Randolph

I shall never forget my mother, for it was she who planted and nurtured the first seeds of good within me. She opened my heart to the lasting impressions of nature; she awakened my understanding and extended my horizon and her precepts exerted an everlasting influence upon the course of my life.

—*Immanuel Kant*

*M*y mother is a woman who speaks with her life as much as with her tongue.

—*Kesaya E. Noda*

$\mathcal{S}$he speaks with wisdom and faithful instruction is on her tongue. She watches over the affairs of her household and does not eat the bread of idleness. Her children arise and call her blessed; her husband also, and he praises her: "Many women do noble things, but you surpass them all."

—*Proverbs 31:26–29*

$\mathcal{Y}$ou can choose your friends, but you only have one mother.

—*Max Shulmon*

Making the decision to have a child is momentous. It is to decide forever to have your heart walking around outside your body.

—*Elizabeth Stone*

Motherhood is not for the fainthearted. Used frogs, skinned knees, and the insults of teenage girls are not meant for the wimpy.

—*Danielle Steele*

$\mathcal{A}$s a mother you become sensitive, not only to all of life's wonders but also to its injustices. You are a more feeling person.

—*Jaclyn Smith*

$\mathcal{B}$eing a mother, as far as I can tell, is a constantly evolving process of adapting to the needs of your child while also changing and growing as a person in your own right.

—*Deborah Insel*

*T*ime is the only comforter for the loss of a mother.

—*Jane Welsh Carlyle*

I cannot forget my mother. Though not as sturdy as others, she is my bridge. When I needed to get across, she steadied herself long enough for me to run across safely.

—*Renita Weems*

No other balm for earthly pain
Is half so sure,
No sweet caress so filled with love
Nor half so pure,
No other soul so close akin that understands,
No touch that brings such perfect
peace as Mother's hands.

—W. Dayton Wedgefarth

$\mathcal{M}$y mother was the most beautiful woman . . . All I am I owe to my mother . . . I attribute all my success in life to the moral, intellectual, and physical education I received from her.

—*George Washington*

$\mathcal{Y}$ou never get over being a child as long as you have a mother to go to.

—*Sarah Orne Jewett*

Loving a child doesn't mean
giving in to all his whims; to love him
is to bring out the best in him, to teach
him to love what is difficult.

—*Nadia Boulanger*

The older I get, the more of my mother I see in myself.

—*Nancy Friday*

I love being able to share my whole life with someone who is a part of me and doesn't criticize me for not being perfect. A child's love is unconditional.

—*Florence Griffith Joyner*

*M*otherhood deepens your connection to all of life, making you a more active participant in both the joys and pains of living. You seek out things in the world that will enhance your child's life and pleasure, becoming a frequent visitor to parks and museums, a reader of books on whales and dinosaurs, an avid eater of ice cream and a singer of songs, a hiker, and a tree climber. You also see the insides of doctors' offices and even hospitals more often than you'd like, stay up later and wake up earlier than you ever care to, and sustain patience even as chaos constantly threatens to erupt around you. It is not always easy, but you can find no greater sense of being fully alive than in what is asked of you in being a mother.

—*Alexandra Stoddard,* MOTHERS: A CELEBRATION

𝒜 mother is a person who, seeing there are only four pieces of pie for five people, promptly announces she never did care for pie.

—*Tenneva Jordan*

𝑀y mother had a great deal of trouble with me, but I think she enjoyed it.

—*Mark Twain*

The more people have studied different methods of bringing up children, the more they have come to the conclusion that what good mothers and fathers instinctively feel like doing for their babies is the best after all.

—*Benjamin Spock*

A mother's heart is an abyss at the bottom of which there is always forgiveness.

—*Honoré De Balzac*

I am fooling myself when I say my mother exists now only in the photograph on my bulletin board or in the outline of my hand or in the armful of memories I still hold tight. She lives on beneath everything I do. Her presence influenced who I was, and her absence influences who I am.

—*Hope Edelman*, MOTHERLESS DAUGHTER

*A*nyone who doesn't miss the past never had a mother.

—*Gregory Nunn*

Who takes the child by the hand
takes the mother by the heart.

—*Danish proverb*

*N*o matter how old a mother is, she watches her middle-aged children for signs of improvement.

—*Florida Scott-Maxwell*

*T*he commonest fallacy among women is that simply having children makes one a mother—which is as absurd as believing that having a piano makes one a musician.

—*Sidney J. Harris*

A mother is not a person to lean on but a person to make leaning unnecessary.

—*Dorothy Canfield Fisher*

*I*t will be gone before you know it. The fingerprints on the wall appear higher and higher. Then suddenly they disappear.

—*Dorothy Evslin*

All women become like their mothers. That is their tragedy. No man does. That is his.

—*Oscar Wilde*

My mother drew a distinction between achievement and success. She said that achievement is the knowledge that you have studied and worked hard and done the best that is in you. Success is being praised by others, and that's nice, too, but not as important or satisfying. Always aim for achievement and forget about success.

—*Helen Hayes*

A good woman is the best thing on earth. Women were last at the cross and first at the open tomb. The church owes a debt to her faithful women which she can never estimate, to say nothing of the debt we owe in our homes to godly wives and mothers.

—*Vance Havner*

𝒴ou have to love your children unselfishly.
That's hard. But it's the only way.

—*Barbara Bush*

𝓜other is the name of God in the lips and
hearts of children.

—*William Makepeace Thackeray*

You may give them your love but not your thoughts,

For they have their own thoughts.

You may house their bodies but not their souls,

For their souls dwell in the house of tomorrow,

Which you cannot visit even in your dreams.

—*Kahlil Gibran*

A man never sees all that his mother has been
to him till it's too late to let her know that he sees it.

—*William Dean Howells*

*T*he mother-child relationship is paradoxical and,
in a sense, tragic. It requires the most intense love
on the mother's side, yet this very love must help the
child grow away from the mother, and to become
fully independent.

—*Erich Fromm*

*I*t is the general rule that all superior men inherit the elements of superiority from their mothers.

—*Jules Michelet*

*T*hey always looked back before turning the corner, for their mother was always at the window to nod and smile and wave her hand at them. Somehow it seemed as if they couldn't have got through the day without that, for whatever their mood might be, the last glimpse of that motherly face was sure to affect them like sunshine.

—*Louisa May Alcott*

I think it must somewhere be written that the virtues of mothers shall be visited on their children, as well as the sins of the fathers.

—*Charles John Huffman*

*T*here are times when parenthood seems nothing but feeding the mouth that bites you.

—*Peter de Vries*

A mother understands what a child does not say.

—*Yiddish proverb*

*T*he best thing to give to your enemy is forgiveness; to an opponent, tolerance; to a friend, your heart; to your child, a good example; to a father, deference; to your mother, conduct that will make her proud of you; to yourself, respect; to all men, charity.

—*Francis Maitland Balfour*

She knew how to make virtues out of necessities.

—*Audre Lorde*

A mother can read all the child-rearing books and can subscribe to any theory of parenting, but what gets passed along to her children is something far more intimate and mysterious than anything contained therein. What gets passed along is her character, and it enters into her kids as surely and as inexorably as water flows from a fuller vessel into a less-full one.

—*Laurence Shames*

$\mathcal{Y}$our children need your presence more than they need your presents.

—*Jesse Jackson*

$\mathcal{M}$otherhood brings as much joy as ever, but it still brings boredom, exhaustion, and sorrow too. Nothing else will ever make us as happy, or as sad, as proud or as tired, for nothing is quite as hard as helping a person develop his own individuality— especially while struggling to keep your own.

—*Marguerite Kelly and Ella Parsons*

*M*y mother had a slender, small body, but a large heart—a heart so large that everybody's grief and everybody's joy found welcome in it, and hospitable accommodation.

—*Mark Twain*

All that I am my mother made me.

—*John Quincy Adams*

When I was a child, my mother said to me, "If you become a soldier, you'll be a general. If you become a monk, you'll end up as the pope." Instead I became a painter and wound up as Picasso.

—*Pablo Picasso*

When the good Lord was creating mothers he was into his sixth day of overtime when the angel appeared and said, "You're doing a lot of fiddling around on this one."

And the Lord said, "Have you read the specs on this order? She has to be completely washable, but not plastic; have 180 moveable parts, all replaceable; run on black coffee and leftovers; have a lap that disappears when she stands up; a kiss that can cure anything from a broken leg to a disappointed love affair; and six pairs of hands."

The angel shook her head slowly and said, "Six pairs of hands . . . no way!"

"It's not the hands that are causing me problems," said the Lord, "It's the three pairs of eyes that mothers have to have."

—*Erma Bombeck's Tribute to Her Mom*

*E*ducation commences at the mother's knee, and every word spoken within the hearing of little children tends towards the formation of character.

—*Hosea Ballou*

*F*allopian tubes and ovaries do not a mother make.

—*Oprah Winfrey*

A father may turn his back on his child, brothers and sisters may become inveterate enemies, husbands may desert their wives, wives their husbands. But a mother's love endures through all.

—*Washington Irving*

It is not until you become a mother that your judgment slowly turns to compassion and understanding.

—*Erma Bombeck*

A true mother is not merely a provider, housekeeper, comforter, or companion. A true mother is primarily and essentially a trainer.

—*Ruth Bell Graham*

When mother reads aloud I long

For noble deeds to do —

To help the right, redeem the wrong,

It seems so easy to be strong,

so simple to be true,

O, thick and fast the visions crowd

When mother reads aloud.

—*Anonymous*

$\mathcal{I}$ looked on child-rearing not only as a work of love and duty but as a profession which was fully as interesting and challenging as any honorable profession in the world.

—*Rose Kennedy*

$\mathcal{S}$ome are kissing mothers and some are scolding mothers, but it is love just the same, and most mothers kiss and scold together.

—*Pearl S. Buck*

*E*very beetle is a gazelle in the eyes of its mother.

—*Moorish proverb*

I used to be a reasonably careless and adventurous person before I had children; now I am morbidly obsessed by seatbelts and constantly afraid that low-flying aircraft will drop on my children's school.

—*Margaret Drabble*

$\mathcal{C}$hildren have more need of models than critics.

—*Joseph Joubert*

$\mathcal{M}$otherhood is being available to your children whenever they need you, no matter what their age or their need.

—*Major Doris Pengilly*

$\mathcal{M}$others, food, love, and career, the four major guilt groups.

—*Cathy Guisewite*

$\mathcal{I}$ think we're seeing in working mothers a change from "Thank God it's Friday" to "Thank God it's Monday." If any working mother has not experienced that feeling, her children are not adolescent.

—*Ann Diehl*

$\mathcal{T}$he house came alive with the sound of slamming doors. Books skidded across the table, coming to rest precariously close to the edge. My eleven-year-old son was home from school. I started to hug him, but resisted the urge. Motherly gestures had become unpopular lately.

"Hey, Mom! Guess what! Mr. Travers, our gym instructor has arranged a camp-out at Bear Lake. Can I go?

"Slow down," I said, my stomach muscles stiffening. "Bear Lake is a long way from here."

"It won't cost a lot, Mom," he continued, ignoring my apprehension. "I'll need a pup tent, but there's my newspaper route. And I could mow lawns."

My mind scrambled for excuses. "I'll think about it," I said.

"I have to know by Friday." His voice was low.

I had three days to consider. Four nights to lie awake and worry. How could I let him go? What if something happened to him?

On Wednesday, Greg mowed the lawn. As usual he left wide swaths of grass uncut around the trees. For some reason the sight reassured me.

On Thursday, Greg and I worked on his school project, a complicated series of switches and buttons and a bell. I had tried to talk him into something simpler, but that was what he wanted to do.

I reached out to hold a wire for him. His fingers were deft as they tightened the nut. And suddenly I noticed that his hands were bigger than mine. I closed my eyes and saw baby fingers struggling with shoelaces. When had Greg's hands become so square and steady and large?

I took a deep breath and touched Greg's shoulder. "I've been wondering." My voice was steady. The fear was gone, though I knew it would come back. I'd have to grapple with it again and again. "Is it too early in the season to shop for a pup tent?"

Understanding burst across his face. "Oh, Mom. Thank you!"

He flung himself at me in a big bear hug. I held him close for just a moment, but lightly this time, ready to let go.

—*Margaret Chittenden, "A Child No More"*

*I*f at first you don't succeed, do it like your mother told you.

—*Anonymous*

We never make sport of religion, politics, race, or mothers. A mother never gets hit with a custard pie. Mothers-in-law—yes. But mothers—never.

—*Mack Sennett*

Nobody loves me but my mother, and she could be jivin' too.

—*B. B. King*

*T*his lesson we shall learn:
A boy's best friend is his mother.

—*Joseph P. Skelley*

*N*o man is poor who has a godly mother.

—*Abraham Lincoln*

*W*ith a mother of different mental caliber I should probably have turned out badly. But her firmness, her sweetness, her goodness were potent powers to keep me in the right path . . . My mother was the making of me.

—*Thomas Edison*

A mother's arms are made of tenderness, and children sleep soundly in them.

—*Victor Hugo*

*T*here never was a child so lovely but his mother was glad to get him asleep.

—*Ralph Waldo Emerson*

*P*eculiar isn't it . . . first you're scolding your children and then all at once they're so smart they're scolding you.

—*Ann Tyler*

*T*here's no question that the mother-daughter relationship is the most complex on earth. It's even more complicated than the man-woman thing.

—*Naomi Judd*

*F*or the mother is and must be, whether she knows it or not, the greatest, strongest, and most lasting teacher her child will have. Other influences come and go, but hers is continual.

—*Hanna Whitall Smith*

*M*y mother, who is my spiritual touchstone, told me to remember three things in life: "You have one body, respect it; one mind, feed it well; and one life—enjoy it."

—*Des'ree*

*W*hen I stopped seeing my mother with the eyes of a child, I saw the woman who helped me give birth to myself.

—*Nancy Friday*

I think my life began with waking up and loving my mother's face.

—*George Eliot*

*J*udicious mothers will always keep in mind that they are the first book read, and the last put aside, in every child's library.

—*C. Lenox Redmond*

The debt of gratitude we owe our mother and father goes forward, not backward. What we owe our parents is the bill presented to us by our children.

—*Nancy Friday*

I am the part of the woman the same as the man,

And I say it is as great to be a woman as to be a man,

And I say there is nothing greater than

the mother of a man.

—*Walt Whitman*

*T*here is nothing more thrilling in this world, I think, than having a child that is yours, and yet is mysteriously a stranger.

—*Agatha Christie*

*W*e never know the love of the parent till we become parents ourselves.

—*Henry Ward Beecher*

In all my efforts to learn to read, my mother shared fully my ambition and sympathized with me and aided me in every way she could. If I have done anything in life worth attention, I feel sure that I inherited the disposition from my mother.

—*Booker T. Washington*

A mother holds her children's hands for a while . . . their hearts forever.

—*Unknown*

Mothers are the place that we call home.

On them we rest our heads and close our eyes.

There's no one else who grants the same soft peace,

Happiness, contentment, sweet release,

Erasing nighttime tears with lullabies,

Restoring the bright sun that makes us bloom.

—*Nicholas Gordon*

*M*ama exhorted her children at every opportunity to 'jump at de sun.' We might not land on the sun, but at least we would get off the ground."

—*Zora Neale Hurston*

*H*uman beings are the only creatures on earth that allow their children to come back home.

—*Bill Cosby*

There is no influence so powerful as that of the mother.

—*Sarah Joseph Hale*

I come from a political family. None of us ever sought public office, but we were schooled in party politics plank by plank. Before I could tie my shoes, I knew that if a Republican candidate's only opponent was a yellow dog, we voted for the yellow dog. My earliest memories were political: voting with Mom, getting to pull the curtain behind us in the boiled-greens-smelling elementary school, watching her decisively cast her ballot, getting a little lecture on the way home about freedom and responsibility, which ended invariably with Mom wisecracking, "You all remember to vote when you grow up, early and often."

Other children asked for "Goodnight Moon," but we asked for political stories, like the backwoods candidates so corrupt they were called Big Evil and Little Evil. I remember coming home to find my mother and our elderly mailman watching the coverage of President Kennedy's assassination, both of them weeping. I remember Dad, who had a civilly disobedient agenda, doing a happy dance when he discovered that a radical southern magazine for which he did artwork had been honored with a spot on Nixon's enemies list.

But my single most significant political lesson came from watching presidential primary returns when I was fifteen and seeing one solitary vote in our all-white precinct for African-American candidate Shirley Chisholm. "Hey, that's me," said Dad, claiming the labors of his political love. Mom, a somewhat more pragmatic McGovern supporter, chided, "You're throwing your vote away." "I vote my conscience," Dad insisted. Though Chisholm's voters barely rippled the political pond, her candidacy and Dad's lone vote impressed upon me like no majority could the importance of making your voice heard.

So I was horrified when I learned that not one student at a nearby state college voted in our presidential primary this year, even though they rated their own campus polling place. Poll watchers sat all day with their coffee and their lists, but no one showed up to cast a ballot. As friends and I discussed our own voting records, I discovered that most of us who vote religiously were taken to the polls as children. I'm a mother now to two liberals in training who regularly accompany me to vote, even though it would be easier to slip to the polls while they're in school. They take turns in a cafeteria that still smells like boiled greens. One of them pulls the handle that shuts the voting booth curtain behind us. They both watch as I flip the red levers. On the way home, I give them my mom's lecture, "Every time there's an election"—and they say, "Early and often."

—*Nancy Hall*

$\mathcal{M}$others all want their sons to grow up to be president, but they don't want them to become politicians in the process.

—*John Fitzgerald Kennedy*

$\mathcal{C}$hildren are likely to live up to what you believe of them.

—*Lady Bird Johnson*

$\mathcal{M}$ost of all the other beautiful things in life come by twos and threes, by dozens and hundreds. Plenty of roses, stars, sunsets, rainbows, brothers and sisters, aunts and cousins, but only one mother in the whole world.

—*Kate Douglas Wiggin*

$\mathcal{M}$other love is the fuel that enables a normal human being to do the impossible.

—*Unknown*

Who fed me from her gentle breast,

And hushed me in her arms to rest

And on my cheek sweet kisses pressed?

My Mother.

When pain and sickness made me cry.

Who gazed upon my heavy eye,

And wept, for fear that I should die?

My Mother.

Who ran to help me when I fell,

and would some pretty story tell,

Or kiss the place to make it well?

My Mother.

And can I ever cease to be

Affectionate and kind to thee,

Who was so very kind to me?

My Mother.

—*Anne Taylor*

A man loves his sweetheart the most, his wife the best, but his mother the longest.

—*Irish Proverb*

*H*onor your father and your mother, that your days may be long . . .

—*Exodus 20:12*

*T*he best thing you can give children, next to good habits, are good memories.

—*Sydney J. Harris*

*M*otherhood is still the biggest gamble in the world. It is the glorious life force. It's huge and scary. It's an act of infinite optimism.

—*Gilda Radner*

*F*or the hand that rocks the cradle is the hand that rocks the world.

—*William Ross Wallace*

$\mathcal{M}$other, your presence hovers everywhere, over house, over garden, over dreams, over silence. You are within me. I'll not lose you.

—*Toby Talbot*

$\mathcal{T}$o a mother, a son is never a fully grown man; and a son is never a fully grown man until he understands and accepts this about his mother.

—*Unknown*

*R*icher than I you can never be—I had a mother who read to me.

—*Strickland Gilliland*

*T*hough motherhood is the most important of all professions—requiring more knowledge than any other department in human affairs—there was no attention given to preparation for this office.

—*Elizabeth Cady Stanton*

When I have extended myself beyond my reach
and come toppling Humpty-Dumpty down on my
face in full view of a scornful world, I have returned to
my mother to be liberated by her one more time . . .
My mother raised me, and then freed me.

—*Maya Angelou*

A little girl, asked where her home was, replied,
"Where mother is."

—*Keith L. Brooks*

James James

Morrison Morrison

Weatherby George Dupree

Took great

Care of his Mother

Though he was only three.

— *A. A. Milne*

$\mathcal{M}$y mother was the making of me. She was so true and so sure of me I felt I had something to live for—someone I must not disappoint. The memory of my mother will always be a blessing to me.

—*Thomas Edison*

$\mathcal{S}$he never quite leaves her children at home, even when she doesn't take them along.

—*Margaret Culkin Banning*

If we never have headaches through rebuking our children, we shall have plenty of heartaches when they grow up.

—*Charles H. Spurgeon*

$\mathscr{M}$others have big aprons—to cover the faults of their children.

—*Jewish Saying*

$\mathscr{T}$he finest inheritance you can give to a child is to allow it to make its own way, completely on its own feet.

—*Isadora Duncan*

In life you may have friends,

fond, dear friends, but never will

you have again the inexpressive

love and gentleness lavished

upon you, which none but

a mother bestows.

—*Thomas Abington McCaulay*

$\mathcal{M}$ama seemed to do only what my father wanted, and yet we lived the way my mother wanted us to live.

—*Lillian Hellman*

$\mathcal{A}$ vacation frequently means that the family goes away for a rest, accompanied by mother, who sees that the others get it.

—*Marcelene Cox*

In the Middle Ages, a custom called *Mothering Sunday* began when children, who often left home early to learn a trade or become apprentices, would be released from work every year on the fourth Sunday of Lent to attend church with their families. As they returned home, they often took cakes or little gifts to their mothers.

It was in 1872 that Julia Ward Howe (author of *The Battle Hymn of the Republic*) suggested the idea of Mother's Day in the United States.

The cause was taken up by Anna Jarvis, daughter of a Methodist pastor. Jarvis felt the scars of the Civil War could be healed by mothers—and by honoring mothers. She died in 1905 before her dream of establishing a holiday could be fulfilled. But her daughter, also named Anna Jarvis, took up the crusade.

Anna had been deeply influenced by her mother, and she often recalled hearing her mother say that she hoped someone would one day establish a memorial for all mothers, living and dead.

Anna had been particularly touched at age twelve while listening to her mother teach a Sunday school class on the subject "Mothers in the Bible." Mrs. Jarvis closed the lesson with a prayer to this effect: *I hope and pray that someone, sometime, will found a memorial mother's day. There are many days for men, but none for mother.*

Anna thus began a campaign to establish a national Mother's Day. She and her supporters began to write a constant stream of letters to ministers, businessmen, politicians, and newspaper editors. She spent a fortune trying to attract attention to her idea and took every opportunity to give speeches, send telegrams, or write articles promoting her cause.

On the second anniversary of her mother's death, May 12, 1907, Anna led a small tribute to her mother at Andrews Methodist Episcopal Church in Gafton, West Virginia. She donated five hundred white carnations, her mother's favorite flower, to be worn by everyone in attendance. On this first Mother's Day service, the pastor used the text, "Woman, behold thy son; Son, behold thy mother" (John 19:26). That same day a special service was held at the Wannamaker Auditorium in Philadelphia, which could seat no more than a third of the fifteen thousand people who showed up.

After that, things began to take off. Various states jumped on the bandwagon, officially proclaiming a

Mother's Day each year, and in 1914, President Woodrow Wilson officially established Mother's Day a national holiday to be held on the second Sunday of May.

God knows that a mother needs fortitude and courage and tolerance and flexibility and patience and firmness and nearly every other brave aspect of the human soul. But because I happen to be a parent of almost fiercely maternal nature, I praise casualness. It seems to me the rarest of virtues. It is useful enough when children are small. It is important to the point of necessity when they are adolescents . . .

—*Phyllis McGinley, "A History of Mother's Day"*

To describe my mother would be to write about a hurricane in its perfect power.

—*Maya Angelou*

A man who has been the indisputable favorite of his mother keeps for life the feeling of a conqueror, that confidence of success that often induces real success.

—*Sigmund Freud*

Years ago my mother said to me, "In this world, Elwood, you must be oh so smart or oh so pleasant." For years I was smart. I recommend pleasant.

—*Elwood P. Dowd (Jimmy Stewart),* HARVEY

My mother's menu consisted of two choices: Take it or leave it.

—*Buddy Hackett*

An ounce of mother is worth a
ton of clergy.

—*Spanish Proverb*

*I*t goes without saying that you should never have more children than you have car windows.

—*Erma Bombeck*

A mother is neither cocky, nor proud, because she knows the school principal may call at any minute to report that her child has just driven a motorcycle through the gymnasium.

—*Mary Kay Blakely*

Don't aim to be an earthly saint,

With eyes fixed on a star,

Just try to be the fellow

That your mother thinks you are.

—Will S. Adkin

$\mathscr{I}$ can remember the first time I had to go to sleep. Mom said, "Steven, time to go to sleep." I said, "But I don't know how." She said, "It's real easy. Just go down to the end of tired and hang a left." So I went down to the end of tired, and just out of curiosity I hung a right. My mother was there, and she said, "I thought I told you to go to sleep."

—*Steven Wright*

$\mathscr{I}$t is better to bind your children to you by respect and gentleness than by fear.

—*Terence*

A mother is the truest friend we have, when friends desert us when troubles thicken around us, still will she cling to us, and endeavor by her kind precepts and counsels to dissipate the clouds of darkness, and cause peace to return to our hearts.

—*Washington Irving*

*T*here never was a woman like her. She was gentle as a dove and brave as a lioness. The memory of my mother and her teachings were, after all, the only capital I had to start life with, and on that capital I have made my way.

—*Andrew Jackson*

*E*veryone can keep house better than her mother, until she tries.

—*Thomas Fuller*

What my mother believed about cooking is that if you worked hard and prospered, someone else would do it for you.

—*Nora Ephron*

Babies don't need fathers, but mothers do. Someone who is taking care of a baby needs to be taken care of.

—*Amy Heckerling*

Women's liberation is just a lot of foolishness. It's the men who are discriminated against. They can't bear children. And no one is likely to do anything about that.

—*Golda Meir*

It takes a hundred men to make an encampment, but one woman can make a home.

—*Robert G. Ingersol*

There is no slave out of heaven like a loving woman; And, of all loving women, there is no such slave as a mother.

—*Henry Ward Beecher*

What do girls do who haven't any mothers to help them through their troubles?

—*Louisa May Alcott*

Being a mother is rewarding to one's female instincts, trying to one's nerves, physically exhausting, emotionally both frustrating and satisfying, and above all, not to be undertaken lightly.

—*Dr. Margaret Raphael*

*I*f you bungle raising your children,
I don't think whatever else you do well
matters very much.

—*Jacqueline Kennedy Onassis*

*A*nd so our mothers and grandmothers have, more often than not, anonymously handed on the creative spark, the seed of the flower they themselves never hoped to see—or like a sealed letter they could not plainly read.

—*Alice Walker*

*C*hildren are a great comfort in your old age, and they help you reach it faster, too.

—*Lionel Kaufman*

TERI WILHELMS • DEBBIE DENTON

M-o-t-h-e-r

M is for the million things she gave me,

O means only that she's growing old,

T is for the tears she shed to save me,

H is for her heart of purest gold;

E is for her eyes, with love-light shining,

R means right, and right she'll always be,

Put them all together, they spell Mother,

A word that means the world to me.

—*Howard Johnson*

You're not famous until my mother has heard of you.

—*Jay Leno*

When we as youngsters would accuse our mother of picking on us, her wise reply was, "All you'll get from strangers is surface pleasantry or indifference. Only someone who loves you will criticize you."

—*Judith Crist*

When you are a mother, you are never really alone in your thoughts. You are connected to your child and to all those who touch your lives. A mother always has to think twice, once for herself and once for her child.

—*Sophia Loren*

There was never a great man who had not a great mother.

—*Olive Schreiner*

The most important thing a father can do for his children is to love their mother.

—*Theodore M. Hesburgh*

My father was poor . . . He thought that with the music there was very little to do, and he thought better to be a carpenter. He was thinking seriously of that for me, but my mother said to him, "This boy has a gift, and it is our duty to follow it." She was a wonderful woman.

—*Pablo Casals*

O wonderful son, that can so astonish a mother!

—*William Shakespeare*

❧

I always tell people that I became a writer not because I went to school but because my mother took me to the library. I wanted to become a writer so I could see my name in the card catalog.

—*Sandra Cisneros*

$\mathcal{P}$erhaps the greatest social service that can be rendered by anybody to this country and to mankind is to bring up a family.

—*George Bernard Shaw*

$\mathcal{I}$nstant availability without continuous presence is probably the best role a mother can play.

—*Lotte Bailyn*

A mother is she who can take the place of all others but whose place no one else can take.

—*Cardinal Mermillod*

Any mother could perform the jobs of several air-traffic controllers with ease.

—*Lisa Alther*

Mama was my greatest teacher, a teacher of compassion, love and fearlessness. If love is sweet as a flower, then my mother is that sweet flower of love.

—*Stevie Wonder*

Three words fall sweetly on my soul,

As music from an angel's lyre,

That bid my spirit spurn control

And upward to its source aspire;

The sweetest sounds to mortals given

Are heard in Mother, Home, and Heaven.

—*William Goldsmith Brown*

$\mathcal{R}$eal mothers know that a child's growth is not measured by height or years or grade . . . It is marked by the progression of Mama to Mommy to Mother.

—*Unknown*

$\mathcal{W}$e can't form our children on our own concepts; we must take them and love them as God gives them to us.

—*Johann Wolfgang von Goethe, "Hermann und Dorothea"*

I really can't come to your party, Mrs. Parker, I can't bear fools."

"That's strange; your mother could."

—*Dorothy Parker*

A mother loves her children even when they least deserve to be loved.

—*Kate Samperi*

*A*ll that I am, or hope to be, I owe to my angel mother.

—*Abraham Lincoln*

*G*rown don't mean nothing to a mother. A child is a child. They get bigger, older, but grown. In my heart it don't mean a thing.

—*Toni Morrison*

*T*here are only two things a child will share willingly—communicable diseases and his mother's age.

—*Benjamin Spock*

*A*t work, you think of the children you have left at home. At home, you think of the work you've left unfinished. Such a struggle is unleashed within yourself. Your heart is rent.

—*Golda Meir*

*B*eing a full-time mother is one of the highest salaried jobs . . . , since the payment is pure love.

—*Mildred B. Vermont*

*N*o ordinary work done by a man is either as hard or as responsible as the work of a woman who is bringing up a family of small children; for upon her time and strength demands are made not only every hour of the day but often every hour of the night.

—*Theodore Roosevelt*

*R*omance fails us—and so do friendships—but the relationship of mother and child remains indelible and indestructible—the strongest bond on earth.

—*Theodor Reik*

A rich child often sits in a poor mother's lap.

—*Spanish Proverb*

*Y*ou can get children off you lap, but you can never get them out of your heart.

—*Unknown*

She was so deeply imbedded in my consciousness that for the first year of school I seem to have believed that each of my teachers was my mother in disguise.

—*Philip Roth*, PORTNOY'S COMPLAINT

The mother's heart is the child's schoolroom.

—*Henry Ward Beecher*

I found out why cats drink out of the toilet. My mother told me it's because it's cold in there. And I'm like: How did my mother know that?

—*Wendy Liebman*

*W*hat feeling is so nice as a child's hand in yours? So small, so soft and warm, like a kitten huddling in the shelter of your clasp.

—*Marjorie Holmes*

Before you were conceived I wanted you

Before you were born I loved you

Before you were here an hour I would die for you

This is the miracle of life.

—*Maureen Hawkins*

The mother loves her child most divinely, not when she surrounds him with comfort and anticipates his wants, but when she resolutely holds him to the highest standards and is content with nothing less than his best.

—*Hamilton Wright Mabie*

Mother's love grows by giving.

—*Charles Lamb*

*E*very mother is like Moses. She does not enter the promised land. She prepares a world she will not see.

—*Pope Paul VI*

*M*other's love is peace. It need not be acquired, it need not be deserved.

—*Erich Fromm*

The soul is healed by being with children.

—*Fyodor Dostoevsky*

She was such a good loving mother, my best friend: oh, who was happier than I when I could still say the dear name "mother," and it was heard, and who can I say it to now?

—*Ludwig von Beethoven*

Men are what their mothers made them.

—*Ralph Waldo Emerson*

A woman who is loved always has success.

—*Vicki Baum*

*B*y and large, mothers and housewives are the only workers who do not have regular time off. They are the great vacationless class.

—*Anne Morrow Lindbergh*

Children aren't happy with nothing to ignore,

And that's what parents were created for.

—*Ogden Nash*

$\mathcal{N}$ow, as always, the most automated appliance in a household is the mother.

—*Beverly Jones*

$\mathcal{C}$leaning you house while your kids are still growing is like shoveling the walk before it stops snowing.

—*Phyllis Diller*

*I*t's easy to pick children whose mothers are good housekeepers; they are usually found in other people's yards.

—*Unknown*

*B*ecause I am a mother, I am capable of being shocked: as I never was when I was not one.

—*Margaret Atwood*

Only mothers can think of the future, because they give birth to it in their children.

—*Maxim Gorky*

A mother becomes a true grandmother the day she stops noticing the terrible things her children do because she is so enchanted with the wonderful things her grandchildren do.

—*Lois Wyse*

*M*ost mothers are instinctive philosophers.

—*Harriet Beecher Stowe*

As a girl my temper often got out of bounds. But one day when I became angry at a friend over some trivial matter, my mother said to me, "Elizabeth, anyone who angers you conquers you."

—*Sister Elizabeth Kenny*

A suburban mother's role is to deliver children obstetrically once, and by car forever after.

—*Peter De Vries*

A small boy invaded the lingerie section of a big department store and shyly presented his problem to the salesclerk. "I want to buy my mom a present of a slip," he said, "but I'm darned if I know what size she wears."

The clerk said, "It would help to know if your mom is short or tall, fat or skinny."

"She's just perfect," beamed the little boy, so the clerk wrapped up a size thirty-four for him.

Two days later Mom came to the store herself and changed it to a size fifty-two.

—"She's Just Perfect"

$\mathcal{M}$y mother never gave up on me. I messed up in school so much they were sending me home, but my mother sent me right back.

—*Denzel Washington*

$\mathcal{A}$ smart mother makes often a better diagnosis than a poor doctor.

—*August Bier*

It is odd how all men develop the notion, as they grow older, that their mothers were wonderful cooks. I have yet to meet a man who will admit that his mother was a kitchen assassin, and nearly poisoned him.

—*Robertson Davies*

Everybody's mother still cares.

—*Lillian Hellman*

$\mathcal{T}$he God to whom little boys say their prayers has a face very like their mother's.

—*James Matthew Barrie*

$\mathcal{A}$ girl is Innocence playing in the mud, Beauty standing on its head, and Motherhood dragging a doll by the foot.

—*Allen Beck*

*H*e that would the daughter win,
must with the mother first begin.

—*English Proverb*

A mother never realizes that her children are no longer children.

—*Holbrook Jackson*

S ometimes the strength of motherhood is greater than natural laws.

—*Barbara Kingsolver*

*Y*ou can learn many things from children. How much patience you have, for instance.

—*Franklin P. Jones*

*I*f you can't hold children in your arms, please hold them in your heart.

—*Mother Clara Hale*

Bitter are the tears of a child: Sweeten them.

Deep are the thoughts of a child: Quiet them.

Sharp is the grief of a child: Take it from him.

Soft is the heart of a child: Do not harden it.

—Pamela Glenconner

*E*ven my mother didn't like me all the time, but she let me come home anyway.

—*Ann Mckay Thompson*

*D*o not join encounter groups. If you enjoy being made to feel inadequate, call your mother.

—*Liz Smith*

The mother is the uncharted servant of the future.

—*Katherine Anthony*

Mother is the name for God on the lips and in the hearts of little children.

—*William Makepeace Thackery*

My first Mom died when I was four. I still miss her, think about her, wonder what life was like in our house when she was alive and well. She had cancer. I have memories of her going to the doctor a lot. I also remember her holding me when I fell out of our hayloft. We had babysitters but no one filled her place in my heart. Finally Dad met another mom for my brother and me who were still home. I was so excited; I was only seven and wanted a mom so bad. We have had our fights, but she loves me and I love her so much. It's been almost thirty-eight years since my Dad married my Mom. She has been there to see me marry, have kids, and go through a bout of breast cancer.

She is in her nineties, so I am trying to prepare myself for the day she won't be there. She took on a lot when she married my Dad, and I'm glad she did. Both my Moms are special to me, and I think of both as my real Mom.

—*Pam Davis*

*M*otherhood is the greatest privilege of life.

—*Mary Roper Coker*

Always there when ever you frown,

And picks you up when you're feeling down,

She's kind and gentle, but sometimes mad,

And you feel upset when she gets sad.

You yell and fight and scream and shout,

You throw a fit and whine and pout,

But you know no matter what you do,

Your mom is always there for you.

She comforts you when times get rough,

And sets you straight when you feel tough,

She knows your weaknesses and your strengths,

And to make you happy would go all lengths.

—*Jenny Parrish*

*M*others are the most important actors in the grand drama of human progress.

—*Elizabeth Cady Stanton*

*O*f all the rights of women, the greatest is to be a mother.

—*Lin Yutang*